People who help us

Teacher

First published in the UK in 2009 by
QED Publishing
A Quarto Group company
226 City Road
London EC1V 2TT
www.qed-publishing.co.uk

A catalogue record for this book is available from
the British Library.

ISBN 978 1 84835 156 1

Printed and bound in China

Author Amanda Askew
Designer and Illustrator Andrew Crowson
Consultants Shirley Bickler and Tracey Dils

Publisher Steve Evans
Creative Director Zeta Davies
Managing Editor Amanda Askew

Words in bold are
explained in the
glossary on page 24.

Teacher

Amanda Askew
Andrew Crowson

QED Publishing

Meet Kimi. She's a teacher at Nuttfield School. She teaches five and six year olds.

When Kimi arrives at the school, Bob the **School Keeper** is sweeping the **playground**.

Carol the **Office Manager** is getting the **registers** ready for the day.

Peter the **Headteacher** is chatting to another teacher.

At 9 o'clock, the pupils arrive and they're noisy!

"Quiet! It's time for the register. Good morning."

"Good morning, Miss Nakata."

Kimi uses a tick for children who are here and an 'A' for **absent** when children are ill.

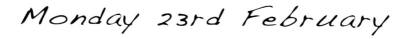

Monday 23rd February

Morning	Numeracy Science
Afternoon	Literacy

"I've written today's **timetable** on the **whiteboard.** This morning, we're going to add money."

"On the table, there are 5ps, 2ps and 1ps. How many different ways can you add them together to make 10p?"

Kimi and Miss Jennings, Kimi's assistant, walk around the room and help the children.

"Miss Nakata, I've finished."
"How many different ways
do you have, Robert?"
"I've found nine ways."
"Well done!"

RING! RING! Playtime! It's raining outside, so Kimi tells the children to play quietly. Jane and Lisa play with their teddies.

Jonathan and Joe build towers with play-bricks.

Claire, Alice and May look at a book about scary animals.

13

After playtime,
Kimi and the
children plant
beans. They fill
a small pot with
soil. Then they
plant a bean
and add water.

"Put some pots next to the window and some in the cupboard. Then we can see which grows best."

RING! RING! Lunchtime!

Kimi eats her lunch with the children. Some children bring lunch from home. Jack has a cheese sandwich, a yoghurt and a banana.

Some children have
school dinners.

May has pasta
with mushrooms,
sweetcorn, ham
and broccoli.

In the afternoon, Kimi reads the children a story.

18

The story is about a mouse that lives in a lighthouse.

"I need to help my friend," Kimi squeaks in her best mouse voice. All the children laugh!

"What do you know about mice?"

"They are very small."
"They have whiskers and a long tail."
"My pet mouse is called Ralph."

"Well done! You've worked very hard today."

"Miss Jennings will put your pictures on the wall and we can sing a song before the bell rings."

"Hickory dickory dock,
the mouse ran up the clock.
The clock struck one,
the mouse ran down,
hickory dickory dock!"

23

Glossary

Absent Not at school.

Headteacher The teacher who is in charge of the school.

Office Manager The person who looks after all the school files and registers.

Playground An area outside where children play.

Register A list of names, so the teacher can check who is at school and who is absent.

School Keeper The person who looks after the school building and makes sure it is clean and tidy.

Timetable A list of what happens each day in a class.

Whiteboard A board on the wall that teachers write on using a special pen.